ERITREA 2016 HUMAN RIGHTS REPORT

EXECUTIVE SUMMARY

Eritrea is a highly centralized, authoritarian regime under the control of President Isaias Afwerki. The People's Front for Democracy and Justice (PFDJ), headed by the president, is the sole political party. There have been no elections since the country's independence from Ethiopia in 1993.

Civilian authorities in the regime generally maintained effective control over most security forces.

The three most important human rights abuses included the inability of citizens to choose their government in free and fair elections; detention without charge under harsh conditions that reportedly sometimes resulted in death; and forced participation in the country's national service program, routinely for periods of indefinite duration beyond the 18-month legal obligation.

Other abuses included killings and disappearances; torture and other cruel, inhuman, and degrading treatment; arbitrary arrest; executive interference in the judiciary; lack of due process and excessively long pretrial detention; politically motivated detentions; evictions without due process; infringement on privacy rights; restrictions on freedom of speech and press; restrictions on academic freedom and cultural events; restrictions on freedom of assembly, association, and religion; limits on freedom of internal movement and foreign travel; corruption and lack of transparency; violence against women and girls; and discrimination against ethnic minorities. The law criminalizes consensual same-sex sexual activity. Female genital mutilation/cutting, human trafficking, and forced labor occurred. Government policies limited worker rights.

The government did not generally prosecute or punish officials who committed abuses, whether in the security services or elsewhere in the government. Impunity was the norm.

Section 1. Respect for the Integrity of the Person, Including Freedom from:

a. Arbitrary Deprivation of Life and other Unlawful or Politically Motivated Killings

The government reportedly committed arbitrary killings with impunity and subjected detainees to harsh and life-threatening prison conditions. Prisoners who disappeared often were presumed dead.

The COI found that authorities had widely committed extrajudicial executions and arbitrary killings since independence. The COI's findings--based on interviews conducted outside of the country (see section 5, United Nations and Other International Bodies)--included extrajudicial killings before the border war of veterans with disabilities and political opponents, including Muslim scholars and others; extrajudicial executions of political opponents, smugglers, and others for less serious or "speculative" crimes; mass killings of members of certain ethnic groups; and systematic execution by the armed forces of soldiers accused of cowardice or desertion during the border war.

The COI found the government, largely the armed forces and particularly the border surveillance division, implemented a shoot-to-kill policy to prevent its citizens from crossing the border into Ethiopia. According to the COI, this policy had been in effect for a "considerable period of time." The COI's June 8 report stated it had "reliable evidence" that the policy still existed but was "not implemented as rigorously as it was in the past."

b. Disappearance

An unknown number of persons disappeared during the year and were believed to be in government detention or to have died while in detention. The government did not regularly notify family members or respond to requests for information regarding the status of detainees, including locally employed staff of foreign embassies or foreign nationals. Disappeared persons included those detained for political and religious beliefs, journalists, individuals suspected of evading national service and militia duties, and persons not known to have committed any offense.

c. Torture and Other Cruel, Inhuman, or Degrading Treatment or Punishment

The law and the unimplemented constitution prohibit torture. According to the COI, the government engaged in the widespread use of torture and other cruel, inhuman, and degrading treatment. The COI found that officials used mistreatment such as extreme forms of restraint, rape, or beatings to cause severe physical and psychological pain during interrogations and to punish detainees and conscripts, and this mistreatment constituted torture. The COI found that officials had either directly ordered torture or it was inflicted with their consent and acquiescence. According to the COI, "The recurrence, coherence, and similarities of the many torture incidents… is a clear indication of the existence of a deliberate policy to inflict torture in a routine manner in the context of investigations and interrogations as well as during national service." The COI received approximately three hundred accounts of torture and mistreatment occurring between 1991 and June 2015.

Lack of transparency and access to information made it impossible to determine the numbers or circumstances of deaths due to torture or poor detention conditions.

Security forces tortured and beat army deserters, national service and militia evaders, persons attempting to flee the country without travel documents, and members of certain religious groups.

The COI reported sexual violence against women and girls was widespread in military training camps, the sexual violence by military personnel in camps and the army amounted to torture, and the forced domestic service of women and girls in training camps amounted to sexual slavery. In a March 2015 report, the Committee on the Elimination of Discrimination against Women (CEDAW) expressed concern regarding reports of women in national service frequently being subjected to sexual violence, including rape.

Prison and Detention Center Conditions

Prison conditions remained harsh and life threatening.

<u>Physical Conditions</u>: There were numerous official and unofficial detention centers, some located in military camps. The law requires juveniles be held separately from adults. There is a juvenile detention center in Asmara, but authorities held some juveniles, particularly teenagers, with adults, due to overcrowding in juvenile facilities. When police arrested mothers, their young children sometimes were held with them. Severe overcrowding was common.

Data on the prevalence of death in prison and detention facilities were not available, although persons reportedly died from harsh conditions, including lack of medical care and use of excessive force. Authorities held some detainees incommunicado in metal shipping containers and underground cells without toilets or beds. Use of psychological torture was common, according to inmates held in prior years. Some former prisoners reported authorities conducted interrogations and beatings within hearing distance of other prisoners to intimidate them. The government did not provide adequate basic or emergency medical care in prisons or detention centers. Food, sanitation, ventilation, and lighting were inadequate, and potable water was sometimes available only for purchase.

Former detainees and other sources reported harsh detention conditions in police stations and in prisons for persons held for evading national service and militia duties.

Authorities placed political prisoners in solitary confinement more often than other detainees (see section 1.d., Political Prisoners and Detainees).

Administration: It was impossible to verify whether authorities released prisoners after they served their sentences. Recordkeeping procedures were not transparent, and the government did not routinely announce the release of prisoners. There were no prison ombudsmen to respond to complaints.

Prisoners and detainees did not have consistent access to visitors. The government did not grant consular access to detained dual-national citizens. Authorities generally did not permit family visits with persons detained, arrested, or convicted for reasons purportedly involving national security but permitted visits with those held for other reasons. Authorities did not permit religious observance for some prisoners and detainees, although at least one detention center had a facility where authorities permitted inmates to conduct religious observances. International religious organizations claimed authorities interrogated detainees regarding their religious affiliation and asked them to identify members of unauthorized religious groups. Prisoners and detainees could not submit complaints to judicial authorities, and authorities did not adequately investigate or monitor prison or detention center conditions.

Independent Monitoring: The government rarely permitted monitoring by independent government or nongovernmental observers. The government did not permit international bodies, including the International Committee of the Red Cross (ICRC), to monitor prison conditions. The government also did not provide the ICRC with information about or access to Ethiopian and Djiboutian prisoners of war detained in the country.

The June 8 COI report noted that in February representatives of the Office of the UN High Commissioner for Human Rights were able to visit the Sembel Prison and Rehabilitation Center. It noted, however, the visit was short and did not allow for a full assessment.

d. Arbitrary Arrest or Detention

The law and unimplemented constitution prohibit arbitrary arrest and detention, but such acts remained widespread.

Mass arrests of persons suspected of evading national service continued.

Role of the Police and Security Apparatus

Police are responsible for maintaining internal security, and the armed forces are responsible for external security, but the government sometimes used the armed forces, the reserves, demobilized soldiers, or the civilian militia to meet domestic and external security requirements. Agents of the National Security Office, which reports to the Office of the President, are responsible for detaining persons suspected of threatening national security. The armed forces have authority to arrest and detain civilians. Police generally do not have a role in cases involving national security.

Impunity for abuse was the norm. There were no known internal or external mechanisms to investigate security force abuse, or government actions to reform the security forces.

Arrest Procedures and Treatment of Detainees

The law stipulates that unless there is a crime in progress, police must conduct an investigation and obtain a warrant prior to making an arrest, but this seldom occurred. In cases involving national security, police may waive the process. Detainees must be brought before a judge within 48 hours of arrest and may not be held more than 28 days without being charged with a crime. Authorities generally detained suspects generally for longer periods without bringing them before a judge, charging them with a crime, or telling them the reason for detention. Authorities sometimes arbitrarily changed charges during detention. The government promoted the assumption that they detained persons held without charge due to national security concerns.

The law provides for a bail system, but bail was arbitrarily denied, bail amounts were capriciously set or not set, and being released on bail sometimes involved paying bribes.

Detainees held on national security grounds did not have access to counsel. Other detainees, including indigent persons, often did not have such access either. Incommunicado detention was widespread. Detainees did not have routine access to visitors. Authorities generally did not permit family visits for persons detained or arrested for reasons purportedly involving national security but usually permitted weekly visits with those held for other reasons.

Arbitrary Arrest: Arbitrary arrest occurred frequently. Security force personnel detained individuals for reasons that included suspicion of intent to evade national and militia service, criticizing the government, attempting to leave the country, and unspecified national security threats. Authorities also continued to arrest members of unregistered Christian groups.

Authorities sometimes arrested persons whose papers were not in order and detained them until they were able to provide evidence of their militia status or demobilization from national service. The government contacted places of employment and used informers to attempt to identify those unwilling to participate in the militia.

There were occasional reports, particularly from rural areas, that security forces detained and interrogated the parents, spouses, or siblings of individuals who evaded national service or fled the country.

Persons arrested in previous years for refusing to bear arms on grounds of conscience and for participating in unregistered religious groups remained in detention.

Pretrial Detention: The government held numerous detainees without charge or due process. Detainees might not be told the reason for their arrest. Authorities brought few, if any, persons detained purportedly on national security grounds to trial. The percentage of the prison and detention center population in pretrial detention was not available.

Detainee's Ability to Challenge Lawfulness of Detention before a Court: Detainees were not able to challenge the lawfulness of detention before a court.

<u>Amnesty</u>: There were reports of dual-national citizens who authorities released after serving their sentences being rearrested days later when they attempted to depart the country.

e. Denial of Fair Public Trial

The law and unimplemented constitution provide for an independent judiciary, but executive control of the judiciary continued, and the judiciary was neither independent nor impartial. Judicial corruption remained a problem. The Office of the President served as a clearinghouse for citizens' petitions to some courts. It also acted as an arbitrator or a facilitator in civil matters for some courts. The judiciary suffered from lack of trained personnel, inadequate funding, and poor infrastructure.

Trial Procedures

The law and unimplemented constitution provide for the presumption of innocence and for defendants to be informed promptly and in detail of charges in a language they understand. The constitution provides for a fair, speedy, and public hearing by a court of law, but it allows the court to exclude the press and public for reasons relating to morals or national security. The law does not specifically address the provision of adequate time or facilities to prepare one's defense, access to government-held evidence, the right of defendants to confront witnesses, or the provision of free interpretation from the moment charged through all appeals, although courts generally accorded these rights to defendants in cases courts did not deem related to national security. There is no right for defendants to refuse to testify.

In civil and criminal courts, defendants have the right to be present and to consult with attorneys or to present their own evidence if they do not wish an attorney. Prosecution and defense lawyers are court appointed and have the right to present evidence and witnesses. Courts of first instance are at the regional level. Each party to a case has the right to one appeal. Decisions rendered by any regional court may be appealed to the next appellate court. Should the appellate court reverse a decision of the lower court, the party whose petition was not sustained may appeal to the five-judge upper appellate court. If the lower appellate court upholds the decision of a regional court, there is no second appeal.

Special courts have jurisdiction over corruption and national security cases. During the year authorities did not try persons detained on national security grounds or for political reasons. Authorities did not inform persons detained on national security grounds of charges against them. Special courts did not protect the rights of defendants. They did not provide defendants with access to a lawyer. Judges serve as prosecutors and may request that individuals involved in cases testify. Special court judges are military officials. The special courts report to the Ministry of Defense and the Office of the President. Trials in special courts are not open to the public, and the court's decisions are final, without appeal.

Community courts headed by elected officials were widely used in rural areas and generally followed traditional and customary law rather than formal law. Local administrators in rural areas encouraged citizens to reconcile outside the court system for less serious cases. Trials in community courts were open to the public and heard by a panel of judges.

In May 2015 the government published revised penal, criminal procedure, civil, and civil procedure codes. The codes had yet to be put into effect by year's end.

Political Prisoners and Detainees

According to Amnesty International, the government held thousands of detainees without charges or trial, including suspected political prisoners and prisoners of conscience, opposition politicians, journalists, members of registered and unregistered religious groups, and persons suspected of not completing national service or evading militia practice. Authorities subjected such persons to harsher treatment in detention than were other detainees. The government did not permit access to detainees by international human rights or humanitarian organizations. The government continued to hold members of the G-15, a group of former ruling party members and officials who called for reforms, and journalists detained in 2001. It did not provide family members with information regarding their well-being or whereabouts.

Civil Judicial Procedures and Remedies

There are no civil judicial procedures for individuals claiming human rights violations by the government.

Property Restitution

The COI noted it received uncorroborated information on continuing demolitions and evictions.

f. Arbitrary or Unlawful Interference with Privacy, Family, Home, or Correspondence

The law and the unimplemented constitution prohibit arbitrary interference with privacy, family, home, or correspondence, but the government did not respect these rights.

Many citizens believed the government monitored cell phones in particular, since authorities required permits to use SIM cards.

The government used an extensive informer system to gather information.

Membership in the PFDJ, the only legal political party, was not mandatory, but authorities pressured some categories of individuals, particularly those occupying government positions, to join the party. Authorities occasionally convoked citizens to attend political indoctrination meetings as part of mandatory participation in the militia irrespective of PFDJ membership. Authorities denied benefits such as ration coupons to those who did not attend. Some citizens in the diaspora claimed convocations occurred at Eritrean embassies, with the names of those who did not attend reported to government officials, sometimes resulting in denial of benefits such as passport services.

Obligatory national service influenced the choices of men and women to marry and have children. Some girls and women married and had children to avoid national service or being mobilized.

There were occasional reports, particularly from rural areas, that security forces detained and interrogated the parents, spouses, or siblings of individuals who evaded national service or fled the country.

Section 2. Respect for Civil Liberties, Including:

a. Freedom of Speech and Press

Although the law and unimplemented constitution provide for freedom of speech and press, the government severely restricted these rights.

<u>Freedom of Speech and Expression</u>: The government severely restricted the ability of individuals to criticize the government in public or in private through intimidation by national security forces.

<u>Press and Media Freedoms</u>: The law bans private broadcast media and foreign ownership of the media and requires that documents, including books, be submitted to the government for approval prior to publication. The government controlled all domestic media, including a newspaper published in three languages, three radio stations, and all local television broadcasters.

The law requires journalists to be licensed. The law restricts printing and publication of materials. The printing of a publication by anyone lacking a permit and the printing or dissemination of prohibited foreign publications are both punishable by law. Government approval is required for distribution of publications from religious or international organizations.

The government permitted satellite dishes that provided access to international cable television networks and programs. The use of satellite dishes was common in Asmara, Massawa, and other cities and increasingly in the countryside. Satellite radio stations operated by diaspora Eritreans reached listeners in the country. Citizens could also receive radio broadcasts originating in Ethiopia.

<u>Violence and Harassment</u>: The government did not provide information on the location or health of journalists it detained in previous years and who were held incommunicado.

<u>Censorship or Content Restrictions</u>: Most independent journalists remained in detention or lived abroad, which limited domestic media criticism of the government. Authorities required journalists to obtain government permission to take photographs. Journalists practiced self-censorship due to fear of government reprisal.

<u>National Security</u>: The government repeatedly asserted national security concerns were the basis of limitations on free speech and expression.

Internet Freedom

The government monitored some internet communications, including e-mail, without obtaining warrants. Government informants frequented internet cafes. The government discouraged citizens from viewing some opposition websites by labeling the sites and their developers as saboteurs. Some citizens expressed fear of arrest if caught viewing such sites. Nonetheless, the sites were generally available.

Eritel, a government-owned corporation, has a monopoly on land-based internet service provision. The use of internet cafes with limited bandwidth in Asmara and other large communities was widespread, but the vast majority of persons did not have access to the internet. According to the most recent data released by the International Telecommunication Union, 1.1 percent of the population used the internet in 2015. Internet users who needed larger bandwidth paid prices beyond the reach of most individuals.

Academic Freedom and Cultural Events

The government restricted academic freedom and cultural events.

Authorities monitored activities at private secondary schools and in some cases arbitrarily denied visas to foreign teachers or presented impediments to school administration, including restricting the import of teaching materials. Some parents of students in private schools charged that educational quality suffered because of disputes between government officials and school administrators.

With few exceptions, secondary school students must complete their final year of high school at the government's Sawa National Training and Education Center. Students had to complete military training at Sawa before being allowed to take entrance exams for institutions of higher education (see section 6, Children).

The government sometimes denied passports or exit visas to students and faculty who wanted to study or do research abroad. The government discouraged students from seeking information on international study and exchange programs and frequently denied them passports or exit visas. Some persons claimed authorities scrutinized academic travel for consistency of intent with government policies.

The government censored film showings and other cultural activities. It monitored libraries and cultural centers maintained by foreign embassies and in some instances questioned employees and users. The government directly sponsored most major cultural events or collaborated with various embassies and foreign cultural institutions in sponsoring musical performances by international performers.

b. Freedom of Peaceful Assembly and Association

Freedom of Assembly

The law and unimplemented constitution provide for freedom of assembly, but the government restricted this right. For some public gatherings, the government intermittently required those assembling to obtain permits. Authorities subjected gatherings of large groups of persons without prior approval to investigation and interference, with the exception of events that occurred in the context of meetings of government-affiliated organizations, were social in nature, or were events such as weddings, funerals, and religious observances of the four officially registered religious groups.

Freedom of Association

Although the law and unimplemented constitution provide for freedom of association, the government did not respect this right. The government did not allow any political parties other than the PFDJ. It also prohibited the formation of civil society organizations except those with official sponsorship. The government generally did not allow local organizations to receive funding and resources from or to associate with foreign and international organizations.

c. Freedom of Religion

See the Department of State's *International Religious Freedom Report* at www.state.gov/religiousfreedomreport/.

d. Freedom of Movement, Internally Displaced Persons, Protection of Refugees, and Stateless Persons

The law and unimplemented constitution provide for freedom of internal movement, foreign travel, emigration, and repatriation, but the government restricted all these rights. It often denied citizens passports and exit visas because they had not completed their military duties or arbitrarily for no given reason.

The government cooperated with the Office of the UN High Commissioner for Refugees (UNHCR) to provide protection and assistance in some areas, but it restricted UNHCR activities in others. The government defined refugee status differently than do the 1951 Convention and 1967 Protocol relating to the Status of Refugees. It did not recognize Ethiopians or Sudanese as refugees, although it allowed them to remain in the country and granted them residency permits. It routinely provided protection to Somali refugees.

UNHCR reported that in May the government halted all resettlement of Somali refugees from the Umkulu Refugee Camp. It ceased issuing exit visas for Somali refugees who were already approved for resettlement in third countries. Additionally, the government prevented Somali refugees in Umkulu from voluntarily repatriating to Somalia, prevented officials from resettlement countries from entering the country to screen additional resettlement candidates, and prevented candidates from exiting the country to be screened in resettlement countries. In November without explanation, the government expelled the UNHCR associate refugee protection officer.

<u>In-country Movement</u>: The government requires citizens to notify local authorities when they change residence, although many did not. When traveling within the country, particularly in remote regions or near borders, authorities required citizens to provide justification for travel at the few checkpoints in the country.

Travel restrictions on noncitizens lawfully in the country remained in effect. The government required all diplomats, international humanitarian workers, UN staff, and foreigners to request permission from the government at least 10 days in advance to travel more than 15.5 miles outside of Asmara. Authorities shortened this waiting period considerably for diplomats who had resided in country for an extended period. Authorities gave UNHCR staff a monthly permit to visit Umkulu Refugee Camp.

<u>Foreign Travel</u>: The government restricted foreign travel. The government required citizens, including dual nationals, to obtain exit visas to depart the country if they entered on an Eritrean passport or residency card. Requirements for obtaining passports and exit visas were inconsistent and nontransparent. Authorities generally did not give exit visas to children ages five and older. Authorities granted few adolescents exit permits; many parents avoided seeking exit permits for children approaching national service draft age due to concern authorities might also deny them permission to travel. Categories of persons most commonly denied exit visas included men under age 54, regardless of whether they had completed the military portion of national service, and women younger than 30, unless they had children. The government did not generally grant exit permits to members of the citizen militia, although some whom authorities demobilized from national service or who had permission from their zone commanders were able to obtain them.

<u>Exile</u>: There were reports of citizens who left the country without exit visas being denied reentry. Many other citizens who fled the country remained in self-imposed exile due to their religious and political views and fear they would be conscripted into national service if they returned. Others reported there were no consequences for returning citizens who had residency or citizenship in other countries.

<u>Emigration and Repatriation</u>: To prevent emigration the government generally did not grant exit visas to entire families or both spouses simultaneously. Authorities arrested persons who tried to cross the border and leave without exit visas.

The COI found the government, largely the armed forces and particularly the border surveillance division, had implemented a shoot-to-kill policy for a "considerable period of time." In its June 8 report, the COI stated that it had "reliable evidence" that the policy still existed, but was "not implemented as rigorously as it was in the past."

In general citizens had the right to return, but citizens residing abroad had to show proof they paid the 2 percent tax on foreign earned income to be eligible for some government services and documents, including exit permits, birth or marriage certificates, passport renewals, and real estate transactions. The government enforced this inconsistently. Persons known to have broken laws abroad, contracted serious contagious diseases, or to have been declared ineligible for political asylum by other governments had their visas and visa requests to enter the country considered with greater scrutiny.

<u>Citizenship</u>: In 1994 the government revoked the citizenship of members of Jehovah's Witnesses due to their refusal to take part in the referendum on independence or participate in the military portion of national service. Members of Jehovah's Witnesses who did not perform military service continued to be unable to obtain official identification documents. They were not eligible for jobs in the formal economy or for ration coupons to buy essentials at government-subsidized prices.

Protection of Refugees

<u>Access to Asylum</u>: The law does not specifically provide for the granting of asylum or refugee status, although the government offered protection to some individuals from neighboring countries, predominantly Somali refugees. The government did not grant Ethiopians or Sudanese asylum, although it allowed them

to remain in the country and granted them residency permits that enabled them to access government services. The government required Ethiopians to pay an annual fee of 600 nakfa ($40) for a residency card. The card demonstrated the holder was not indigent.

Employment: There did not appear to be discrimination based on nationality in terms of employment or entitlements with the exception of resident Ethiopians, some of whom the government viewed as potential security risks.

Access to Basic Services: Persons of Ethiopian and Sudanese origin living in the country sometimes claimed they received social entitlements commensurate with the perceived degree of their loyalty to the government, including eligibility for ration coupons to buy essentials at government-subsidized prices. Most Somalis were restricted to Umkulu Refugee Camp.

Ethiopians and Somalis were able to access basic government services upon procuring and presenting residency permits. UNHCR reported significant delays in the issuance of exit visas for Somali refugees in Umkulu Refugee Camp that caused it to raise concerns with the government regarding the implementation of durable solutions.

Durable Solutions: The government did not grant persons of Ethiopian and Sudanese origin asylum or refugee status; however, authorities permitted them to remain in the country and to live among the local population instead of in a refugee camp. Authorities granted them granted residency permits that enabled them to access government services. Authorities granted Sudanese and Ethiopians exit visas to leave the country for resettlement and study.

Section 3. Freedom to Participate in the Political Process

The law and unimplemented constitution provide citizens the ability to choose their government in free and fair elections, based on universal and equal suffrage and conducted by secret ballot, but they were not able to exercise this ability.

Elections and Political Participation

Recent Elections: The government came to power in a 1993 popular referendum, in which voters chose to have an independent country managed by a transitional government. This government did not permit the formation of a democratic system. The government twice scheduled elections in accordance with the constitution but canceled them without explanation. An official declaration in 2003 asserted, "In accordance with the prevailing wish of the people, it is not the time to establish political parties, and discussion of the establishment has been postponed."

Political Parties and Political Participation: The country is a one-party state. Political power rested with the PFDJ and its institutions. At times the government coerced persons to join the PFDJ.

Participation of Women and Minorities: There are no laws limiting the participation of women and minorities in the political process and women and minorities did so. Women held three of 17 ministerial positions: justice, tourism, and health. Women also served in other government positions, including as ambassador to France and as regional administrators.

Members of ethnic minorities served on the PFDJ's Executive Council and the Central Council. Some senior government and party officials were members of minority groups. The head of the navy was an ethnic Afar.

Section 4. Corruption and Lack of Transparency in Government

The law provides criminal penalties for corruption by officials, but the government did not implement the law effectively, and officials frequently engaged in corrupt practices with impunity. The government, however, reportedly removed some officials from office on grounds of corruption.

The September report of the UN Monitoring Group on Somalia and Eritrea stated, "During past mandates, the Group reported on the roles of Eritrean State officials and the leading figures of the People's Front for Democracy and Justice in controlling public financial management in Eritrea… Interviews conducted by the Group during the current mandate indicate no change in the situation." The group's October 2015 report stated, "The complete lack of financial transparency by the Government of Eritrea enables it to maintain a PFDJ-controlled informal economy. Senior officials in the government and the PFDJ continue to exert full economic control over revenue through a clandestine network of state-owned companies."

Corruption: Persons seeking executive or judicial services sometimes reported they obtained services more easily after paying a "gift" or bribe. Patronage, cronyism, and petty corruption within the executive branch were based largely on family connections and used to facilitate access to social benefits. Judicial corruption was a problem, and authorities generally did not prosecute acts such as property seizure by military or security officials or those seen as being in favor with the government. Reports indicated corruption also existed in the issuance of identification and travel documents, including in the passport office. Individuals requesting exit visas or passports sometimes had to pay bribes.

Amnesty International received reports that soldiers or military vehicles were involved in smuggling persons out of the country.

There were reports of police corruption. Police occasionally used their influence to facilitate the release from prison of friends and family members. Police demanded bribes to release detainees.

Financial Disclosure: The law did not subject public officials to financial disclosure.

Public Access to Information: Although the law and unimplemented constitution provide for public access to government information, the government did not as a rule release statistics or other information to either citizens or noncitizens. There were reports that the government delayed or withheld clearance for the publication of credible information about the effectiveness of government agencies and programs collected by international organizations and nongovernmental organizations (NGOs).

Section 5. Governmental Attitude Regarding International and Nongovernmental Investigation of Alleged Violations of Human Rights

During the years after 2001, the government closed all international NGOs and since then has controlled all local civil society institutions and prevented most international organizations from operating in the country.

The United Nations or Other International Bodies: The government did not permit visits by the UN Commission of Inquiry on Human Rights in Eritrea, the UN special rapporteur on human rights in Eritrea, or the UN Monitoring Group on Somalia and Eritrea.

The government permitted the ICRC to operate but limited its operations to supporting Ethiopian repatriation and vulnerable Ethiopian residents, implementing assistance projects (water, agriculture, and livestock) for persons living in the regions affected by conflict, disseminating information on international humanitarian law to students and government officials, and connecting separated family members living abroad to their family members in the country through the country's Red Cross. Authorities did not permit the ICRC to visit prisons or detention centers.

Section 6. Discrimination, Societal Abuses, and Trafficking in Persons

Women

Rape and Domestic Violence: Rape is a crime punishable by up to 10 years in prison if convicted. Conviction of gang rape or rape of a minor or an invalid is punishable by up to 15 years in prison. Conviction of sexual assault is punishable by six months to eight years in prison. The law does not specifically criminalize spousal rape. No information was available on the prevalence of rape, which citizens seldom reported to officials.

The COI reported sexual violence against women and girls was widespread in military training camps, the sexual violence by military personnel in camps and the army amounted to torture, and the forced domestic service of women and girls in training camps amounted to forced sexual slavery. In a March 2015 report, CEDAW expressed concern about reports that women in national service frequently were subjected to sexual violence, including rape.

Domestic violence is punishable as assault and battery. Domestic violence was commonplace, but such cases rarely were reported or brought to trial. Women usually refrained from openly discussing domestic violence because of societal pressures. Authorities rarely intervened, due to societal attitudes, a lack of trained personnel, and inadequate funding. Traditional authorities, families, or clergy more commonly addressed incidents of domestic violence.

Female Genital Mutilation/Cutting (FGM/C): The law prohibits FGM/C. According to the UN Children's Fund, the prevalence of FGM/C was in decline. Health-care professionals and international organizations reported that the practice continued in several rural areas of the country. The 2010 Population and Health Survey found older cohorts had a higher prevalence of FGM/C than did younger cohorts. The UN Population Fund (UNFPA) worked with the government and other organizations, including the National Union of Eritrean Women and the National Union of Eritrean Youth and Students, on a variety of education programs to discourage the practice.

<u>Sexual Harassment</u>: There is no specific law against sexual harassment. Cultural norms often prevented women from reporting such incidents. There was no record of any person ever being charged or prosecuted for sexual harassment.

<u>Reproductive Rights</u>: The unimplemented constitution provides men and women the legal right to found a family freely. Couples and individuals have the right to decide the number, spacing, and timing of their children, but they often lacked the information, means, and access to do so, free from discrimination, coercion, and violence. Some girls and women married at an early age in order to avoid national service or being mobilized.

According to the World Health Organization, the maternal death rate was an estimated 501 maternal deaths per 100,000 live births, and a woman had a lifetime risk of maternal death of one in 43 as of 2015. The high maternal death rate was likely due to factors including limited health-care services, particularly in rural areas, and adolescent pregnancy. The UN Population Division estimated in 2015 that 15.5 percent of girls and women between ages 15 and 49 used a modern method of contraception. The UNFPA reported that 25 percent of women ages 20-24 had given birth before age 18, based on the most recent data available from 2010. According to the 2010 Population and Health Survey, skilled health-care personnel attended 34 percent of births in the five years preceding the survey. Access to government-provided contraception, skilled health-care attendance during pregnancy and childbirth, prenatal care, essential obstetric care, and postpartum care was available, but women in remote regions sometimes did not seek or could not obtain the care they needed due to lack of spousal or family consent, transport, or awareness of availability.

<u>Discrimination</u>: Family, labor, property, nationality, and inheritance laws provide men and women the same status and rights. The law requires equal pay for equal work. Nevertheless, the percentage of men with access to secondary and higher education, employment, economic resources, property, inheritance, agricultural services, internet connectivity, and other technology exceeded that of women, particularly in rural areas.

Children

<u>Birth Registration</u>: A child derives citizenship from having at least one citizen parent, whether the person is born in the country or abroad. Registration of a birth within the first three months requires only a hospital certificate. After three

months parents must present themselves to judicial authorities with their child and three witnesses. CEDAW reported that authorities registered almost all children born in urban hospitals but not those born in rural areas, where there were few hospitals. If not registered a child may not attend school but may receive medical treatment at hospitals. There were reports of local officials refusing to register the births of children who had a parent living abroad who did not pay the 2 percent tax on foreign earned income.

Education: Education through grade seven is compulsory and tuition-free, although students' families were responsible for providing uniforms, supplies, and transportation. Access to education was not universal. In rural areas parents enrolled fewer daughters than sons in school, but the percentage of girls in school continued to increase.

The government requires all students who reach grade 12 to complete their secondary education at the Sawa National Education and Training Center. Students who did not do so could not graduate and, therefore, could not pursue higher education, although they could attend vocational schools. Some persons who attempted to leave the country did so to avoid going to Sawa because of obligatory military training and poor living conditions at the school.

Child Abuse: Information on the extent of violence against or abuse of children was not available. Local social welfare teams investigated circumstances reported to be abusive and counseled families when child abuse was evident. Society generally accepted physical punishment of children, particularly in rural areas.

Early and Forced Marriage: The legal minimum age for marriage for both men and women is 18, although religious entities may condone marriages at younger ages. According to the 2010 Population and Health Survey, 41 percent of women ages 20-24 were married before 18 and 13 percent before 15. Girls in rural areas were particularly at risk for early marriage. The government encouraged various semiofficial associations such as the National Union of Eritrean Women and the National Eritrean Youth and Student Association to discuss the effect of early marriage and raise awareness among youth regarding its negative consequences. Female ministers spoke publicly on the dangers of early marriage and collaborated with UN agencies to educate the public regarding these dangers, and many neighborhood committees actively discouraged the practice. In June the government and the United Nations launched a national campaign to end child marriage in the country.

<u>Female Genital Mutilation/Cutting (FGM/C)</u>: Information is provided in women's subsection above.

<u>Sexual Exploitation of Children</u>: The law criminalizes child prostitution and includes penalties relating to obscene or indecent publications. The minimum age for consensual sex is 18. Penalties for conviction of the commercial sexual exploitation of children include imprisonment. Crimes were seldom reported, and punishment rarely applied. Data on the extent of child prostitution were not available.

<u>Child Soldiers</u>: The law prohibits the recruitment of children under age 18 into the armed forces. Children under age 18, however, were detained during round-ups and sent to Sawa National Training and Education Center, which is both an educational and military training school. Both the COI and Amnesty International reported on living conditions in Sawa, including insufficient food and health care, and very little family contact. Those who refused to attend and participate in military training either hid, fled the country, or were arrested.

<u>International Child Abductions</u>: The country is not a party to the 1980 Hague Convention on the Civil Aspects of International Child Abduction. See the Department of State's *Annual Report on International Parental Child Abduction* at travel.state.gov/content/childabduction/en/legal/compliance.html.

Anti-Semitism

There were no reports of anti-Semitic acts, and the country's sole remaining Jew maintained the sole synagogue.

Trafficking in Persons

See the Department of State's *Trafficking in Persons Report* at www.state.gov/j/tip/rls/tiprpt/.

Persons with Disabilities

The law and unimplemented constitution prohibit discrimination against persons with disabilities in employment, education, or in the provision of other state services. There are no laws on discrimination in air travel and other transportation, in access to health care, or access to the judicial system. The unimplemented constitution and law do not specify the types of disabilities against which

discrimination is prohibited. The government did not effectively enforce
prohibitions, although it implemented programs to assist persons with disabilities,
especially combat veterans. The government dedicated substantial resources to
support and train thousands of persons with physical disabilities. No laws mandate
access for persons with disabilities to public or private buildings, information, and
communications. There were separate schools for children with hearing, vision,
mental, and intellectual disabilities. Most of these schools were private. The
government provided some support to them. Information on whether there were
patterns of abuse in educational and mental health facilities was not available. The
Ministry of Labor and Human Welfare is responsible for protecting the rights of
persons with disabilities, including mental disabilities.

National/Racial/Ethnic Minorities

Governmental and societal discrimination continued against ethnic minorities,
particularly against the nomadic Kunama and the Afar, two of nine ethnic groups
in the country.

According to a diaspora report, the government detained members of the Kunama
ethnic group.

**Acts of Violence, Discrimination, and Other Abuses Based on Sexual
Orientation and Gender Identity**

The law criminalizes consensual same-sex sexual activity, which is punishable if
convicted by 10 days' to three years' incarceration. The government did not
actively enforce this law. Antidiscrimination laws relating to lesbian, gay,
bisexual, transgender, and intersex (LGBTI) persons do not exist.

There are no hate crime laws or other criminal justice mechanisms to investigate
bias-motivated crimes against LGBTI persons. There was no official action to
investigate and punish those complicit in abuses, including state or nonstate actors.
There were no known LGBTI organizations in the country. In general, society
stigmatized discussion of LGBTI matters.

Section 7. Worker Rights

a. Freedom of Association and the Right to Collective Bargaining

The law provides for the right of workers to form and join independent unions, bargain collectively, and conduct legal strikes. The law prohibits antiunion discrimination and requires reinstatement of union leaders dismissed for union activity, but it does not provide equivalent protection for other workers dismissed for engaging in union activity. The law allows unions to be established in workplaces with at least 20 employees and requires a minimum of 15 members to form a union. The law requires prior authorization from the Ministry of Labor and Human Welfare to establish a union, but it deems registration granted if no response is received from the ministry within one month.

The government did not effectively enforce the applicable laws. While there is a fine for antiunion discrimination or acts of interference, this fine did not constitute an adequate deterrent, according to the International Labor Organization. No corresponding penal law provisions specifically address labor violations.

The government did not respect freedom of association and the right to collective bargaining. Authorities did not allow nongovernmental meetings of more than seven persons. There were no reports of strikes, collective bargaining, or government opposition to, or approval of, the formation of labor associations during the year. Unions existed as governmental organizations for hotel workers, service personnel, agricultural professionals, and teachers, among other occupations. They were ineffective in promoting or protecting workers rights.

In general the government prohibited the operation of NGOs, and no NGOs played a significant role in promoting the rights of workers in the country.

b. Prohibition of Forced or Compulsory Labor

The law prohibits forced labor and slavery but allows compulsory labor for convicted prisoners. The law's definition of forced labor excludes activities performed as part of national service or other civic obligations, and labor protections limiting hours of work and prohibiting harsh conditions did not apply to persons engaged in national service. The law provides penalties of five to 20 years' imprisonment for conviction of "enslavement." The law also provides penalties of imprisonment and fines for "violation of the right to freedom to work," which appears to cover situations of forced labor. The government enforced these laws within private industry.

By law all citizens between ages 18 and 50 must perform national service, with limited exceptions. The national service obligation consists of six months of military training and 12 months of active military service and development tasks in the military forces for a total of 18 months, or for those unfit to undergo military training, 18 months of service in any public and government organ according to the person's capacity and profession. There is no provision for alternative service for conscientious objectors.

Forced labor occurred. Despite the 18-month legal limit on national service, the government did not demobilize many conscripts from the military as scheduled and forced some to serve indefinitely under threats of detention, torture, or punishment of their families. Persons performing national service could not resign or take other employment, generally received no promotions or salary increases, and could rarely leave the country legally because authorities denied them passports or exit visas. Those conscripted into the national service performed standard patrols and border monitoring in addition to labor such as agricultural terracing, planting, road maintenance, hotel work, teaching, construction, and laying power lines.

The government required persons not already in the military to attend civilian militia training and carry firearms, including many who were demobilized, the elderly, or persons otherwise exempted from military service in the past. Failure to participate in the militia or national service could result in detention. Militia duties mostly involved security-related activities, such as airport or neighborhood patrolling. Militia training involved occasional marches and listening to patriotic lectures.

Also see the Department of State's *Trafficking in Persons Report* at www.state.gov/j/tip/rls/tiprpt/.

c. Prohibition of Child Labor and Minimum Age for Employment

The legal minimum age for employment is 14, although this restriction does not apply to self-employed workers. The law prohibits those under age 18 from employment in hazardous categories, including transport industries, work connected with toxic chemicals or dangerous machinery, or work underground or in sewers. This restriction does not apply to apprentices working under supervision. The government prohibits persons under age 18 from employment between 6 p.m. and 6 a.m. and for more than seven hours per day.

Labor inspectors from the Ministry of Labor and Human Welfare are responsible for enforcing child labor laws, but inspections were infrequent and penalties, if imposed, arbitrary. Although the government had a national action plan to protect children from exploitation in the workplace, it did not enforce the plan effectively.

Child labor was widespread in the country. Children in rural areas commonly worked on family farms, fetched firewood or water, and herded livestock. In urban areas children worked as street vendors of cigarettes, newspapers, and chewing gum. Children also worked in small-scale garages, bicycle repair shops, metal workshops, and tea and coffee shops. They also transported grain or other goods via donkey cart or bicycle. Child domestic service occurred. Data on the extent of child prostitution were not available, but it was not visible in Asmara. Begging by children occurred.

The government continued to require secondary school students in the ninth, 10th, and 11th grades to participate in summer work programs known as "maetot." News reports indicated students engaged in activities such as environmental conservation, agricultural activities (irrigation, maintenance of canals, and terracing), and production and maintenance of school furniture. There was no apparent punishment for not participating.

Also see the Department of Labor's *Findings on the Worst Forms of Child Labor* at www.dol.gov/ilab/reports/child-labor/findings/.

d. Discrimination with Respect to Employment and Occupation

With respect to employment and occupation, labor laws prohibit discrimination based on race, color, sex, disability, social origin, nationality, political orientation, or religion. The law does not prohibit discrimination on the basis of sexual orientation or gender identity, HIV-positive status, language, or age. The government did not effectively enforce the laws.

Discrimination against women was common in the workplace and occurred in an environment of impunity. There is no legal prohibition against sexual harassment (see section 6, Women).

e. Acceptable Conditions of Work

The national minimum wage for employees of PFDJ-owned enterprises and government employees was 360 nakfa per month. At the official exchange rate, this equaled $24 (15 nakfa per dollar), but it was considerably less at the unofficial market rate. There was no national minimum wage for private-sector workers.

The government paid national service recruits according to a fixed scale, and the most common salary was 800 nakfa ($53) per month. The standard workweek was 44.5 hours, but employers sometimes required overtime without fair compensation. There were no prohibitions against excessive overtime. The law entitles workers to overtime pay, except for those employed in national service, but this was not always enforced. The legal rest period is one day per week, although most employees received one and one-half days.

No published occupational health and safety standards existed. The Ministry of Labor and Human Welfare is responsible for worker safety and welfare. The ministry employed inspectors, but the number was unclear. No regular enforcement mechanisms were in place, and no inspections of factories occurred to determine whether safety equipment was in use.

Approximately 80 percent of the population was employed in subsistence farming and small-scale retail trading. There were no reliable data on the informal economy and no effective mechanisms for monitoring conditions or protecting workers in the informal economy.

Information regarding abuses pertaining to wage, overtime, safety, and health standards was neither reported nor available.